MathFlare

Name: ______________________

Class: __________

Teacher: ______________________

Introduction

As parents and educators, we recognize the pivotal role mathematics plays in shaping a child's academic journey and future success. Yet, the path to mathematical proficiency can often seem daunting, fraught with challenges and complexities. That's where the transformative power of MathFlare Workbooks shine through, illuminating the way forward with clarity, precision, and purpose.

Introducing MathFlare Workbooks – a beacon of guidance, a testament to excellence, and a catalyst for achievement. Crafted with meticulous care and expertise, MathFlare Workbooks stand as paragons of educational excellence, designed to nurture young minds, ignite a passion for learning, and develop a deep-rooted understanding of mathematical concepts.

Picture this: your child eagerly delves into the pages of Mathflare Workbook, greeted by a step-by-step guide illuminated with vivid examples that demystify complex mathematical concepts. With each turn of the page, they embark on a journey of discovery, encountering thoughtfully curated practice questions that reinforce learning and hone problem-solving skills. And when they unveil the answers to those very questions, a sense of accomplishment blossoms within them – a tangible reward for their hard work and dedication.

But MathFlare Workbooks are more than just tools for learning; they are pathways to comprehension, fostering a deep-seated understanding of mathematical concepts through a sequential, logical flow. From fundamental principles to advanced problem-solving strategies, every chapter builds upon the last, ensuring a robust foundation upon which future knowledge can be constructed.

As parents, we yearn for nothing more than to see our children thrive, to witness the spark of inspiration ignited within them as they conquer academic challenges with confidence and poise. MathFlare Workbooks serve as partners in this noble endeavor, offering not just practice questions, but the keys to unlocking a world of opportunity.

And for teachers, MathFlare Workbooks stand as invaluable allies in the quest to cultivate mathematical proficiency in the classroom. With answers readily available, instructors can focus on guiding and nurturing their students, confident in the knowledge that MathFlare Workbooks provide a solid framework upon which to build.

In the pages of MathFlare Workbooks, we find not just the promise of academic excellence, but the seeds of a brighter tomorrow. So let us embrace the power of mathematics, let us champion the journey of learning, and let us pave the way for a generation of young minds poised to shape the world. With MathFlare Workbooks as our guide, the possibilities are infinite, and the future, bright.

Table of Contents

MathFlare
Grade 2
MATH WORKBOOK
Step by Step Guide and Essential Practice with Answers
Addition Subtraction
Multiplication
Place Value and Expanded Notations
Geometry
MathFlare Publishing

MathFlare
Grade 2-3
MATH WORKBOOK
Step by Step Guide and Essential Practice with Answers
Addition Subtraction
Multiplication and Division
Place Value and Expanded Notations
Geometry
MathFlare Publishing

MathFlare
Grade 3
MATH WORKBOOK
Step by Step Guide and Essential Practice with Answers
Multiplication and Division
Decimals
Place Value and Expanded Notations
Fractions and Geometry
MathFlare Publishing

MathFlare
Grade 1
MATH WORKBOOK
Step by Step Guide and Essential Practice with Answers
Counting and Numbers
Addition and Subtraction
Place Value and Expanded Notations
Understanding Time
MathFlare Publishing

MathFlare
Grade 1-2
MATH WORKBOOK
Step by Step Guide and Essential Practice with Answers
Counting and Numbers
Addition and Subtraction
Place Value and Expanded Notations
Understanding Time
MathFlare Publishing

MathFlare
Grade 3-4
MATH WORKBOOK
Step by Step Guide and Essential Practice with Answers
Addition Subtraction
Multiplication Division
Place Value and Expanded Notations
Fractions and Geometry
MathFlare Publishing

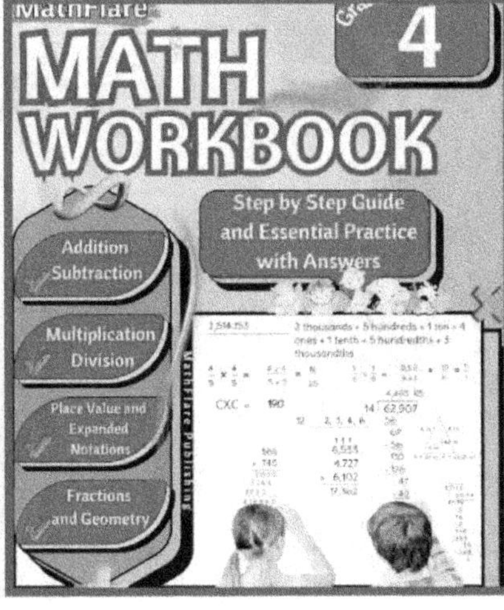
MathFlare
Grade 4
MATH WORKBOOK
Step by Step Guide and Essential Practice with Answers
Addition Subtraction
Multiplication Division
Place Value and Expanded Notations
Fractions and Geometry
MathFlare Publishing

MathFlare
Grade 4-5
MATH WORKBOOK
Step by Step Guide and Essential Practice with Answers
Multiplication Division
Place Value and Expanded Notations
Fractions and Geometry
Unit Conversion
MathFlare Publishing

MathFlare
MATH
WORKBOOK
Grade 5
Step by Step Guide
and Essential Practice
with Answers
Multiplication Division
Place Value and Expanded Notations
Fractions and Geometry
Unit Conversion
MathFlare Publishing

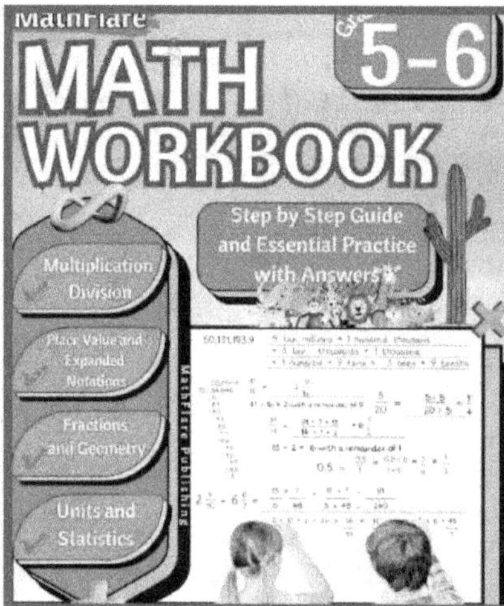

MathFlare
MATH
WORKBOOK
Grade 5-6
Step by Step Guide
and Essential Practice
with Answers
Multiplication Division
Place Value and Expanded Notations
Fractions and Geometry
Units and Statistics
MathFlare Publishing

MathFlare
MATH
WORKBOOK
Grade 6
Step by Step Guide
and Essential Practice
with Answers
Integers and Statistics
Arithmetic and Pre-Algebra
Fractions and Geometry
Ratio and Percentage
MathFlare Publishing

MathFlare
MATH
WORKBOOK
Grade 6-7
Step by Step Guide
and Essential Practice
with Answers
Arithmetic and Pre-Algebra
Ratio, Percent Proportion
Geometry
Statistics
MathFlare Publishing

MathFlare
MATH
WORKBOOK
Grade 7
Step by Step Guide
and Essential Practice
with Answers
Pre-Algebra
Ratio, Percent Proportion
Geometry
Statistics
MathFlare Publishing

MathFlare
MATH
WORKBOOK
Grade 7-8
Step by Step Guide
and Essential Practice
with Answers
Pre-Algebra
Ratio, Percent Proportion
Geometry and Cartesian Plane
Statistics
MathFlare Publishing

MathFlare
MATH
WORKBOOK
Grade 8-9
Step by Step Guide
and Essential Practice
with Answers
Pre-Algebra
Ratio, Proportion and Percentage
Linear Equations
Geometry and Cartesian Plane
MathFlare Publishing

MathFlare
MATH
WORKBOOK
Grade 8
Step by Step Guide
and Essential Practice
with Answers
Pre-Algebra
Percentage
Linear Equations
Geometry
MathFlare Publishing

Multiplication and Division

Multiplication

Multiplication is an easy way of adding numbers together quickly. Instead of adding the same number repeatedly, we use multiplication to find the total much faster.

For instance, rather than adding 2 + 2 + 2 + 2 + 2, we can multiply 2 by 5 to get the same result: 2 x 5 = 10.

Here, the first number (2) is called the multiplicand, second number (5) is the multiplier. The answer we get, in this case, 10, is called the product.

Let's think of multiplication as repeated addition.

Take 2 x 5, for example. It means adding 2 together five times, which we can illustrate as: 2 + 2 + 2 + 2 + 2 = 10

Multiplication can also be visualized as groups of objects. Imagine we have 2 groups, each containing 5 oranges.

To find the total number of oranges, we multiply the number of groups (2) by the number of oranges in each group (5):

2 groups of 5 oranges = 10 oranges

Expressed as multiplication: 2 x 5 = 10

In summary, multiplication offers various ways to approach it: through repeated addition or by envisioning groups of objects. It's a powerful tool that makes solving math problems much quicker and more efficient!

We can also use the following table to quickly remember multiplication facts. The intersection of two points shows the product of two numbers.

For instance, the product of 5 x 6 = 30, or 6 x 5 = 30.

	1	2	3	4	5	6	7	8	9	10
1	1	2	3	4	5	6	7	8	9	10
2	2	4	6	8	10	12	14	16	18	20
3	3	6	9	12	15	18	21	24	27	30
4	4	8	12	16	20	24	28	32	36	40
5	5	10	15	20	25	30	35	40	45	50
6	6	12	18	24	30	36	42	48	54	60
7	7	14	21	28	35	42	49	56	63	70
8	8	16	24	32	40	48	56	64	72	80
9	9	18	27	36	45	54	63	72	81	90
10	10	20	30	40	50	60	70	80	90	100

Let's solve problems from exercises:

$$
\begin{array}{r}
1{,}202 \\
\times \quad\;\; 4 \\
\hline
4{,}808
\end{array}
\qquad
\begin{array}{r}
83 \\
\times\; 86 \\
\hline
498 \\
+664 \\
\hline
7138
\end{array}
\qquad
\begin{array}{r}
552 \\
\times\; 908 \\
\hline
4416 \\
0000 \\
4968 \\
\hline
501216
\end{array}
$$

Commutative Property of Multiplication

The commutative property of multiplication is a special rule in math that tells us the order of the numbers being multiplied doesn't affect the result.

For instance, let's take 2 x 5. If we switch the order of the numbers, multiplying 5 by 2 instead, we'll still end up with the same answer: 2 x 5 = 10, or 5 x 2 = 10.

So, whether we multiply 2 by 5 or 5 by 2, we get 10. That's the commutative property of multiplication in action!

Division

Division is like the opposite of multiplication. It's all about sharing or distributing items equally among a certain number of groups or people.

When we divide one number by another, we're essentially splitting a number into equal parts. We're figuring out how many groups of a certain size can be made from that number.

For instance, let's divide 20 by 4.

When we divide 20 by 4, we're essentially asking, "How many groups of size 4 can we make from 20?"

Now, there are several parts or terms involved in the division process:

- **Dividend:** This is the number being divided, which in this case, is 20.

- **Divisor:** This is the number we're dividing by, which is 4.

- **Quotient:** This is the answer we get after dividing. It tells us how many groups of divisors can be made from the dividend. In this case, the answer is 5.

So, when we divide 20 by 4, we found out that 5 groups of 4 can be made from 20.

Let's solve problems from exercises:

$$
\begin{array}{r}
477 \\
6\overline{)2{,}862} \\
-24 \\
\hline
46 \\
-42 \\
\hline
42 \\
-42 \\
\hline
0
\end{array}
$$

$$
\begin{array}{r}
42 \\
12\overline{)504} \\
-48 \\
\hline
24 \\
-24 \\
\hline
0
\end{array}
$$

$$
\begin{array}{r}
4 \\
4\overline{)16} \\
-16 \\
\hline
0
\end{array}
$$

Multiplication and Division Word Problem:

Anthony can run four laps in 1 hour. How many laps can Anthony run in 18 hours?

$$
\begin{array}{r}
4 \\
\times 18 \\
\hline
+32 \\
+4 \\
\hline
=72
\end{array}
$$

1 hour 4 laps

how many laps can he run in 18 hours?

Anthony can run 72 laps in 18 hours

How many 12 cm pieces of rope can you cut from a rope that is 420 cm long?

$$
\begin{array}{r}
35 \\
12\overline{)520} \\
-36 \\
\hline
60 \\
-60 \\
\hline
0
\end{array}
$$

35 pieces can be cut

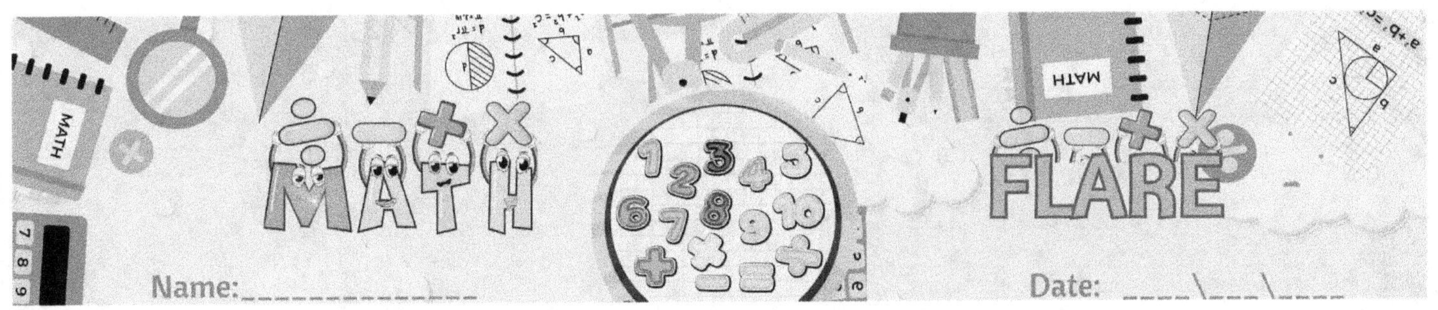

Multiplication: 2 x 1

Find the product.

1. 32 × 1	2. 32 × 3	3. 11 × 2	4. 35 × 1
5. 44 × 2	6. 11 × 4	7. 41 × 2	8. 21 × 4
9. 20 × 2	10. 23 × 2	11. 43 × 2	12. 12 × 4
13. 10 × 5	14. 38 × 1	15. 21 × 3	16. 10 × 2
17. 22 × 4	18. 11 × 5	19. 39 × 1	20. 10 × 4

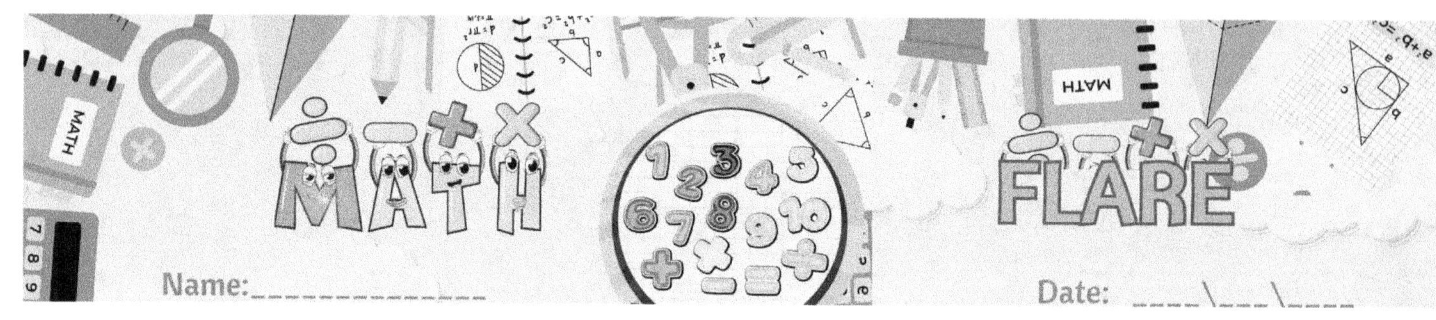

21. 31 × 2	22. 10 × 3	23. 34 × 2	24. 30 × 3
25. 23 × 3	26. 20 × 4	27. 21 × 2	28. 12 × 3
29. 44 × 1	30. 89 × 1	31. 22 × 1	32. 22 × 2
33. 22 × 3	34. 12 × 2	35. 32 × 2	36. 13 × 2
37. 30 × 2	38. 24 × 2	39. 46 × 1	40. 13 × 1

Multiplication: 3 x 1

Find the product.

41. $\quad$ 403 $\times$ 2	42. $\quad$ 206 $\times$ 1	43. $\quad$ 312 $\times$ 2	44. $\quad$ 123 $\times$ 2
45. $\quad$ 104 $\times$ 1	46. $\quad$ 131 $\times$ 3	47. $\quad$ 220 $\times$ 4	48. $\quad$ 121 $\times$ 4
49. $\quad$ 111 $\times$ 5	50. $\quad$ 213 $\times$ 3	51. $\quad$ 132 $\times$ 1	52. $\quad$ 146 $\times$ 1
53. $\quad$ 323 $\times$ 3	54. $\quad$ 203 $\times$ 3	55. $\quad$ 670 $\times$ 1	56. $\quad$ 237 $\times$ 1
57. $\quad$ 112 $\times$ 4	58. $\quad$ 130 $\times$ 3	59. $\quad$ 242 $\times$ 2	60. $\quad$ 211 $\times$ 4

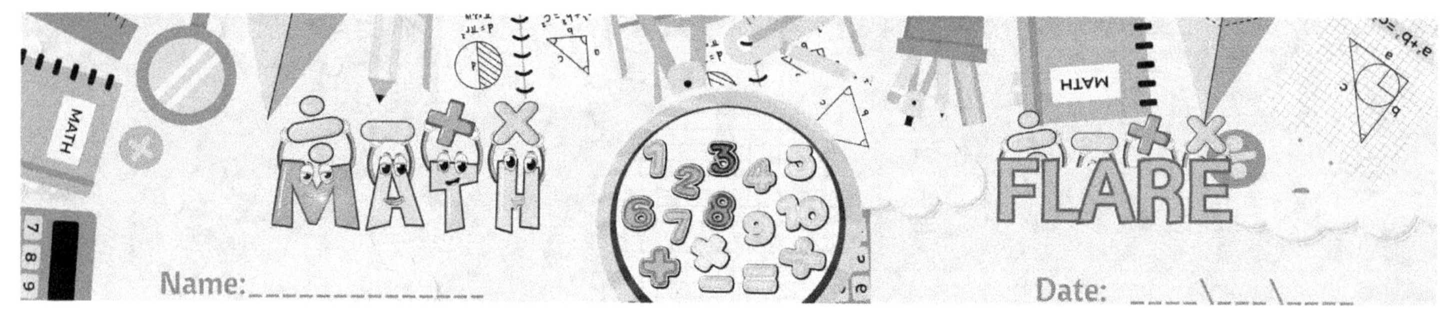

61. 100 × 5	62. 444 × 2	63. 222 × 4	64. 321 × 3
65. 404 × 1	66. 110 × 4	67. 635 × 1	68. 232 × 2
69. 324 × 2	70. 200 × 4	71. 123 × 3	72. 141 × 2
73. 221 × 4	74. 322 × 3	75. 210 × 3	76. 212 × 2
77. 101 × 3	78. 120 × 3	79. 101 × 4	80. 132 × 3

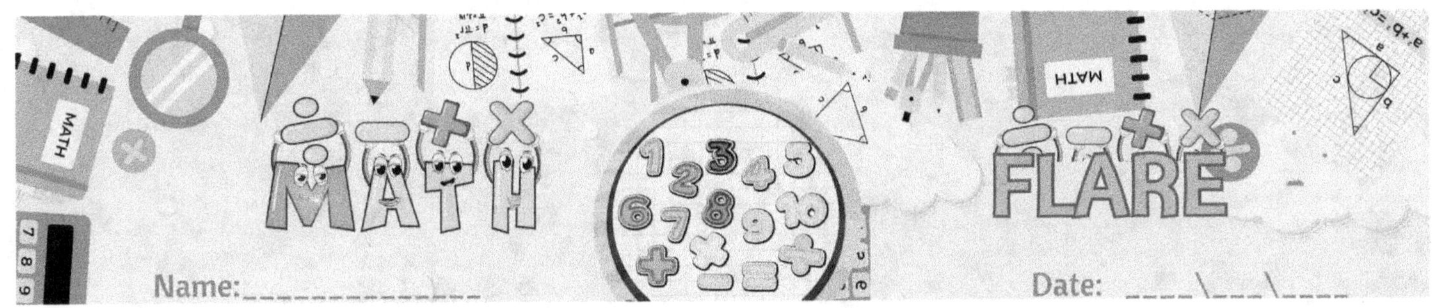

Multiplication: 4 x 1

Find the product.

81. 2,101 × 4	82. 2,314 × 2	83. 1,000 × 3	84. 2,421 × 2
85. 1,202 × 4	86. 7,332 × 1	87. 1,220 × 4	88. 4,131 × 2
89. 4,172 × 1	90. 2,444 × 2	91. 4,124 × 2	92. 1,020 × 4
93. 5,984 × 1	94. 9,870 × 1	95. 1,101 × 4	96. 1,002 × 3
97. 2,122 × 4	98. 4,010 × 2	99. 1,210 × 4	100. 2,210 × 4

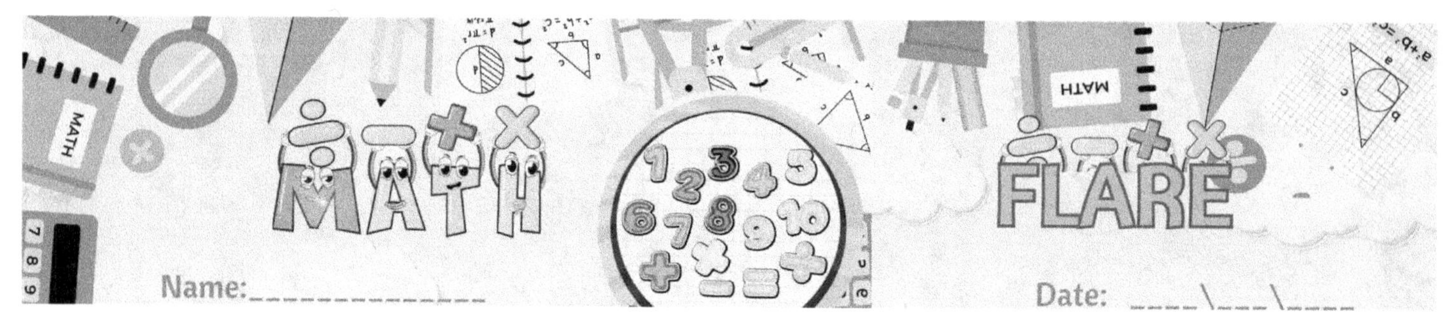

| 101. | 2,021 × 4 | 102. | 2,211 × 4 | 103. | 2,023 × 3 | 104. | 1,011 × 5 |

101. 2,021 × 4
102. 2,211 × 4
103. 2,023 × 3
104. 1,011 × 5

105. 1,011 × 3
106. 2,123 × 2
107. 1,100 × 5
108. 1,113 × 3

109. 1,230 × 2
110. 1,310 × 3
111. 1,331 × 3
112. 3,401 × 2

113. 1,000 × 5
114. 1,120 × 4
115. 2,022 × 3
116. 2,343 × 2

117. 2,102 × 4
118. 4,042 × 2
119. 2,214 × 2
120. 4,344 × 2

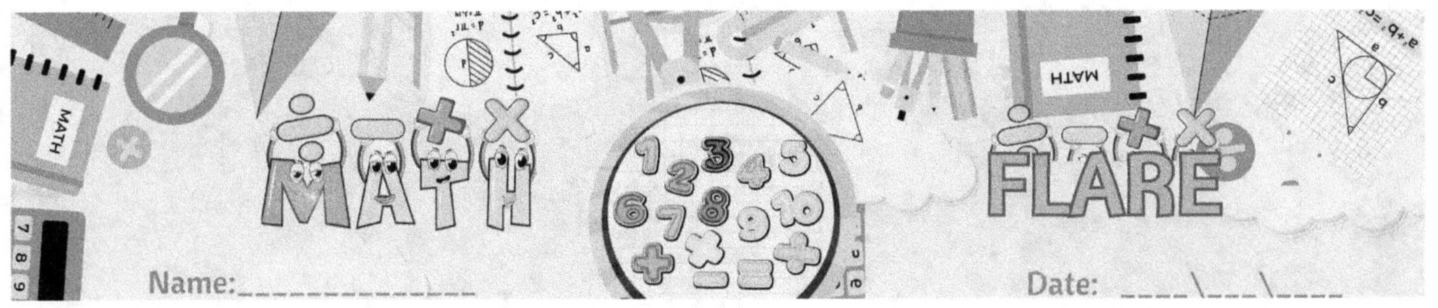

Multiplication (double Digit)

Find the product.

121. 48 × 17	122. 13 × 82	123. 12 × 23	124. 37 × 28
125. 25 × 25	126. 49 × 70	127. 94 × 79	128. 49 × 71
129. 56 × 77	130. 85 × 33	131. 27 × 54	132. 44 × 74

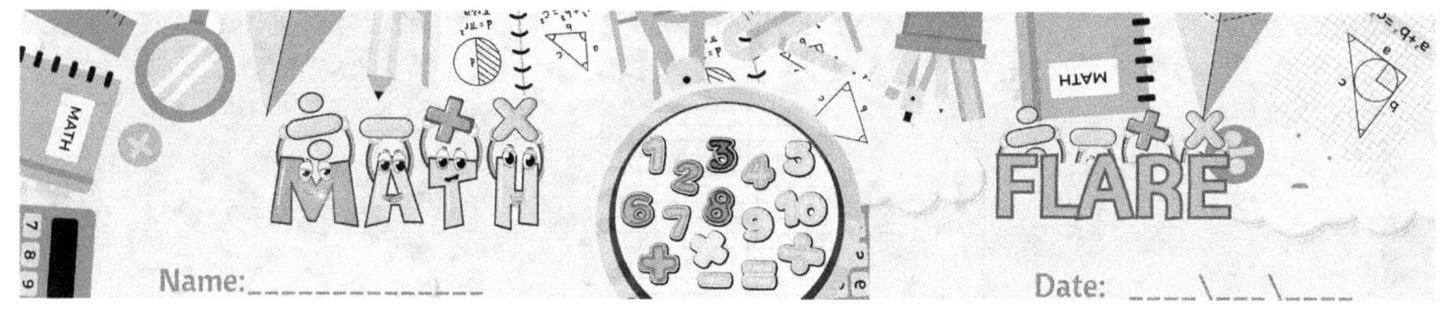

133. $\begin{array}{r} 65 \\ \times\ 62 \\ \hline \end{array}$	134. $\begin{array}{r} 34 \\ \times\ 30 \\ \hline \end{array}$	135. $\begin{array}{r} 91 \\ \times\ 46 \\ \hline \end{array}$	136. $\begin{array}{r} 21 \\ \times\ 33 \\ \hline \end{array}$
137. $\begin{array}{r} 47 \\ \times\ 41 \\ \hline \end{array}$	138. $\begin{array}{r} 85 \\ \times\ 78 \\ \hline \end{array}$	139. $\begin{array}{r} 13 \\ \times\ 52 \\ \hline \end{array}$	140. $\begin{array}{r} 74 \\ \times\ 77 \\ \hline \end{array}$
141. $\begin{array}{r} 63 \\ \times\ 41 \\ \hline \end{array}$	142. $\begin{array}{r} 32 \\ \times\ 34 \\ \hline \end{array}$	143. $\begin{array}{r} 58 \\ \times\ 57 \\ \hline \end{array}$	144. $\begin{array}{r} 21 \\ \times\ 26 \\ \hline \end{array}$
145. $\begin{array}{r} 48 \\ \times\ 59 \\ \hline \end{array}$	146. $\begin{array}{r} 67 \\ \times\ 48 \\ \hline \end{array}$	147. $\begin{array}{r} 27 \\ \times\ 55 \\ \hline \end{array}$	148. $\begin{array}{r} 13 \\ \times\ 92 \\ \hline \end{array}$

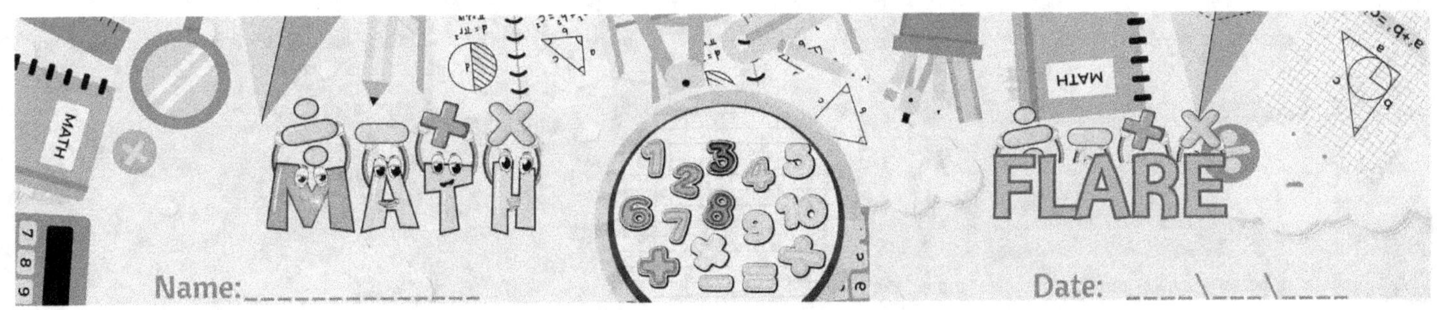

149. 72 × 38	150. 27 × 49	151. 88 × 17	152. 36 × 78
153. 14 × 26	154. 33 × 63	155. 93 × 70	156. 67 × 14
157. 13 × 19	158. 69 × 85	159. 33 × 19	160. 26 × 18
161. 51 × 18	162. 81 × 42	163. 78 × 72	164. 16 × 91

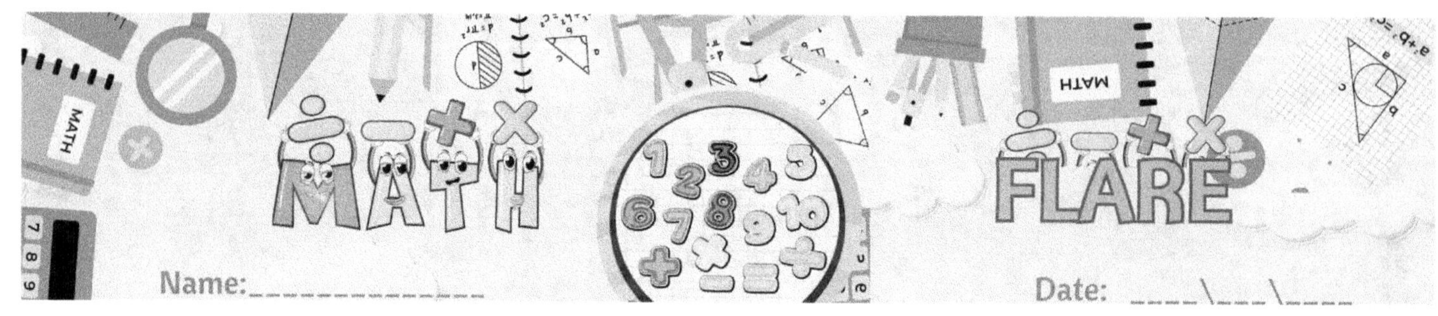

165. $\begin{array}{r} 38 \\ \times\ 92 \\ \hline \end{array}$	166. $\begin{array}{r} 16 \\ \times\ 74 \\ \hline \end{array}$	167. $\begin{array}{r} 35 \\ \times\ 35 \\ \hline \end{array}$	168. $\begin{array}{r} 88 \\ \times\ 56 \\ \hline \end{array}$
169. $\begin{array}{r} 15 \\ \times\ 53 \\ \hline \end{array}$	170. $\begin{array}{r} 30 \\ \times\ 42 \\ \hline \end{array}$	171. $\begin{array}{r} 34 \\ \times\ 57 \\ \hline \end{array}$	172. $\begin{array}{r} 32 \\ \times\ 77 \\ \hline \end{array}$
173. $\begin{array}{r} 91 \\ \times\ 63 \\ \hline \end{array}$	174. $\begin{array}{r} 45 \\ \times\ 18 \\ \hline \end{array}$	175. $\begin{array}{r} 84 \\ \times\ 27 \\ \hline \end{array}$	176. $\begin{array}{r} 70 \\ \times\ 63 \\ \hline \end{array}$
177. $\begin{array}{r} 22 \\ \times\ 19 \\ \hline \end{array}$	178. $\begin{array}{r} 98 \\ \times\ 80 \\ \hline \end{array}$	179. $\begin{array}{r} 35 \\ \times\ 93 \\ \hline \end{array}$	180. $\begin{array}{r} 10 \\ \times\ 41 \\ \hline \end{array}$

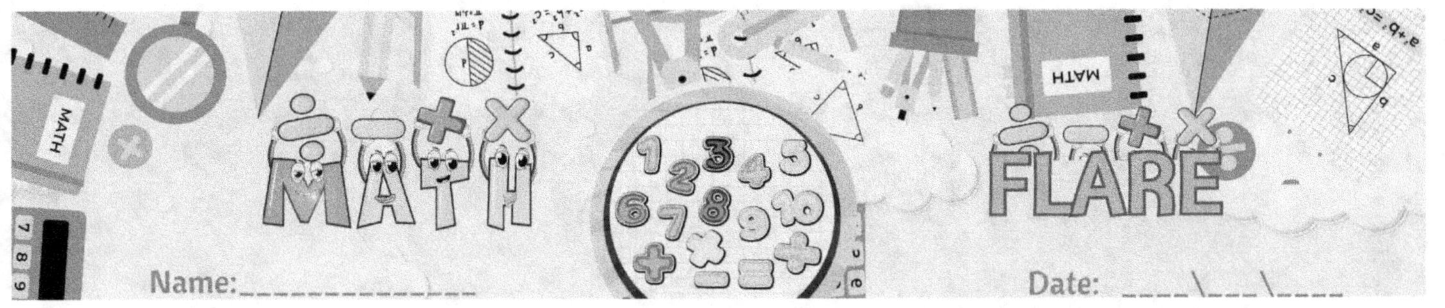

181.	182.	183.	184.
20 × 40	35 × 12	64 × 92	78 × 77

185.	186.	187.	188.
30 × 23	80 × 79	88 × 83	83 × 93

189.	190.	191.	192.
85 × 14	50 × 25	37 × 97	17 × 21

193.	194.	195.	196.
32 × 52	63 × 26	36 × 18	31 × 21

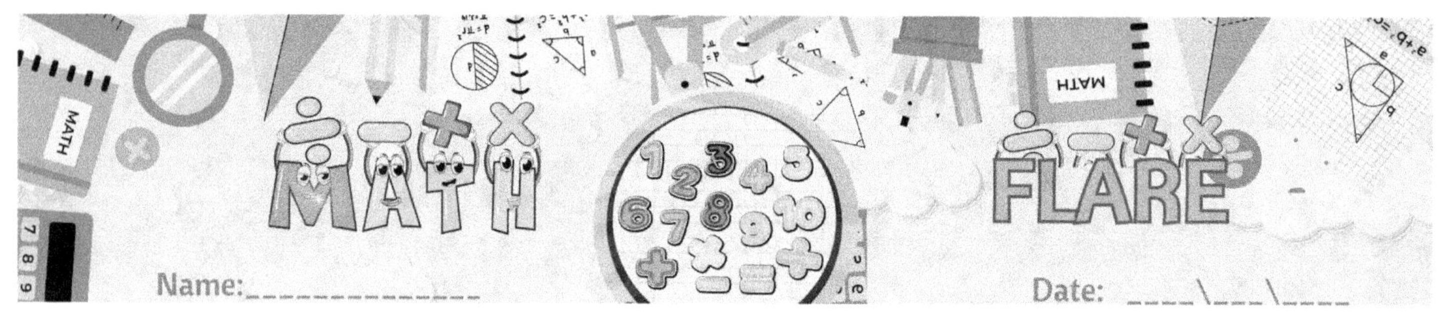

Multiplication (3 Digit)

Find the product.

197. 527
    × 889

198. 323
    × 933

199. 316
    × 303

200. 223
    × 994

201. 854
    × 677

202. 880
    × 718

203. 458
    × 903

204. 745
    × 378

205. 352
    × 145

206. 940
    × 305

207. 532
    × 855

208. 143
    × 222

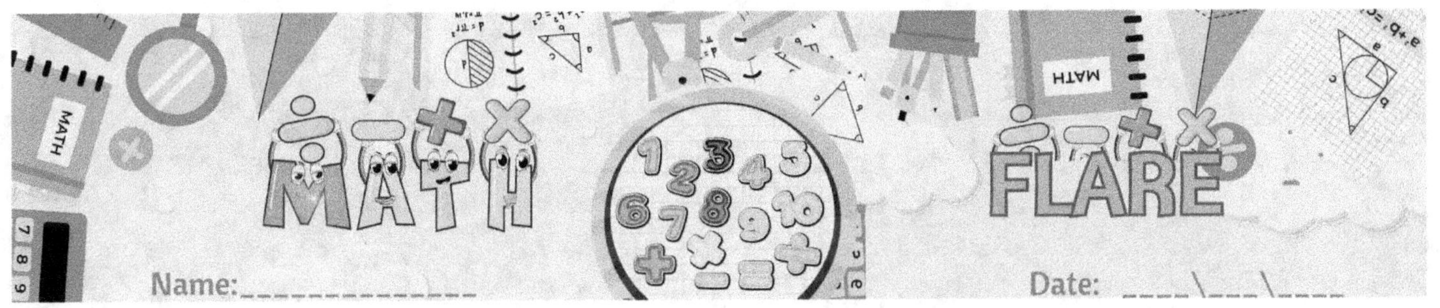

209.   336
  × 240
	210. 795
	  × 230
		211. 393
		  × 621
			212. 516
			  × 218

213.   915
  × 697
	214. 372
	  × 102
		215. 616
		  × 905
			216. 724
			  × 659

217.   920
  × 508
	218. 392
	  × 693
		219. 198
		  × 454
			220. 756
			  × 417

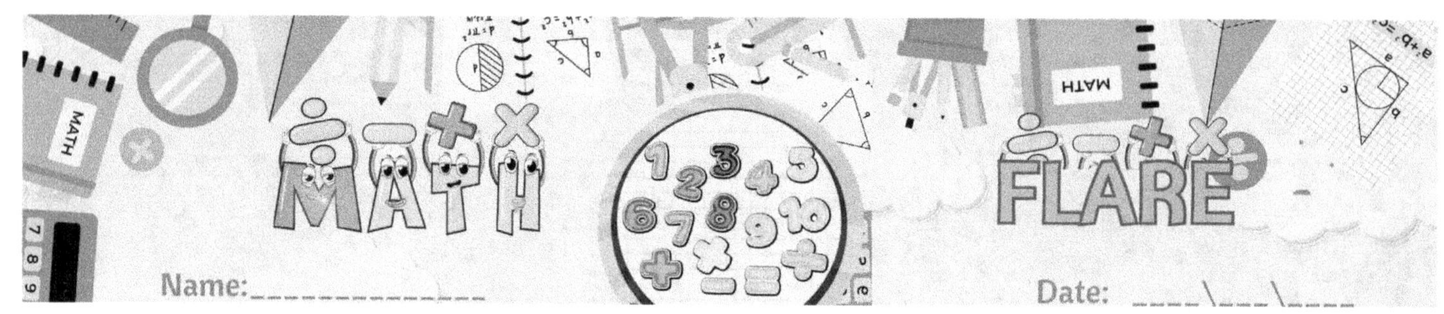

221. 774 × 354	222. 910 × 317	223. 242 × 112	224. 680 × 670
225. 846 × 201	226. 697 × 176	227. 507 × 992	228. 700 × 334
229. 261 × 763	230. 801 × 759	231. 631 × 743	232. 762 × 446

233. 419 × 381

234. 384 × 124

235. 564 × 449

236. 125 × 881

237. 484 × 477

238. 455 × 139

239. 710 × 299

240. 975 × 904

241. 117 × 701

242. 255 × 515

243. 308 × 649

244. 251 × 927

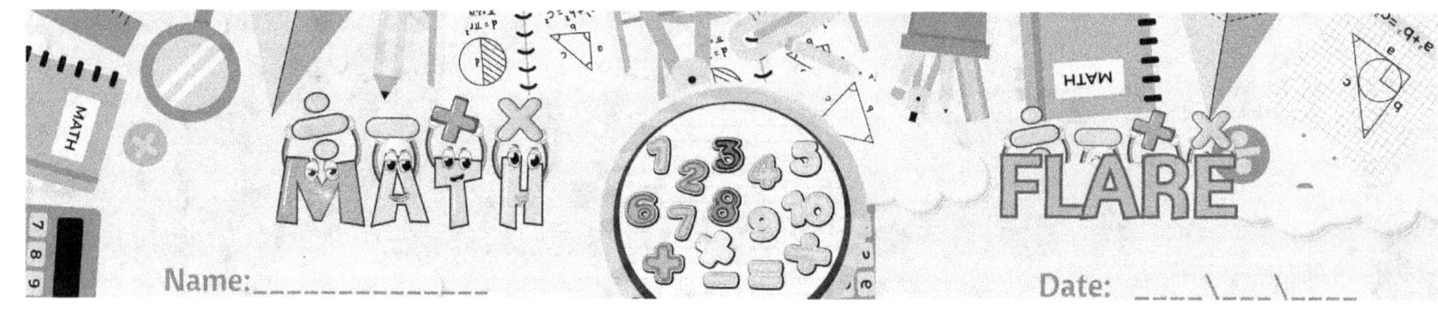

245. 807
    × 158

246. 532
    × 434

247. 651
    × 996

248. 785
    × 131

249. 591
    × 564

250. 897
    × 860

251. 726
    × 656

252. 207
    × 497

253. 177
    × 815

254. 691
    × 130

255. 637
    × 661

256. 623
    × 961

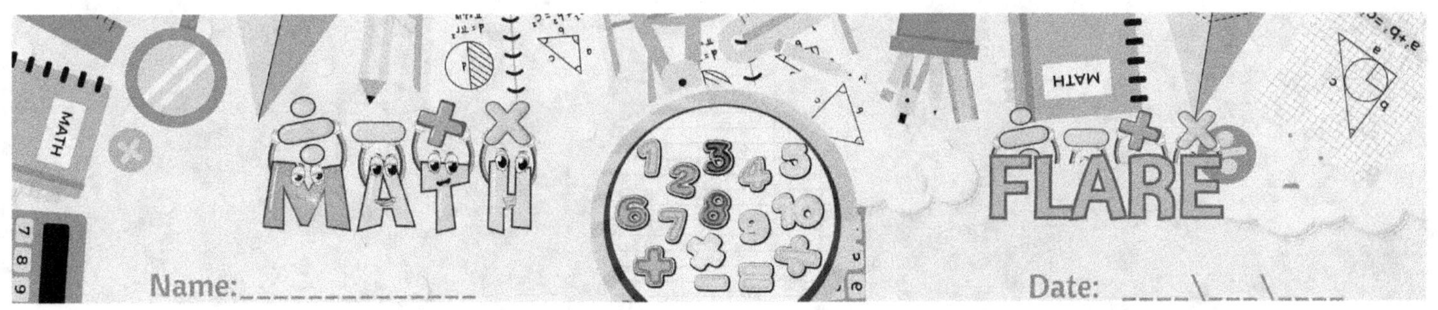

257. 787
    × 897

258. 742
    × 929

259. 588
    × 347

260. 238
    × 770

261. 230
    × 456

262. 316
    × 506

263. 916
    × 690

264. 330
    × 487

265. 691
    × 424

266. 547
    × 246

267. 401
    × 215

268. 277
    × 461

269. $\begin{array}{r} 594 \\ \times\ 758 \\ \hline \end{array}$	270. $\begin{array}{r} 438 \\ \times\ 491 \\ \hline \end{array}$	271. $\begin{array}{r} 957 \\ \times\ 222 \\ \hline \end{array}$	272. $\begin{array}{r} 390 \\ \times\ 246 \\ \hline \end{array}$
273. $\begin{array}{r} 534 \\ \times\ 570 \\ \hline \end{array}$	274. $\begin{array}{r} 646 \\ \times\ 753 \\ \hline \end{array}$	275. $\begin{array}{r} 354 \\ \times\ 855 \\ \hline \end{array}$	276. $\begin{array}{r} 542 \\ \times\ 344 \\ \hline \end{array}$
277. $\begin{array}{r} 426 \\ \times\ 227 \\ \hline \end{array}$	278. $\begin{array}{r} 730 \\ \times\ 370 \\ \hline \end{array}$	279. $\begin{array}{r} 439 \\ \times\ 700 \\ \hline \end{array}$	280. $\begin{array}{r} 579 \\ \times\ 486 \\ \hline \end{array}$

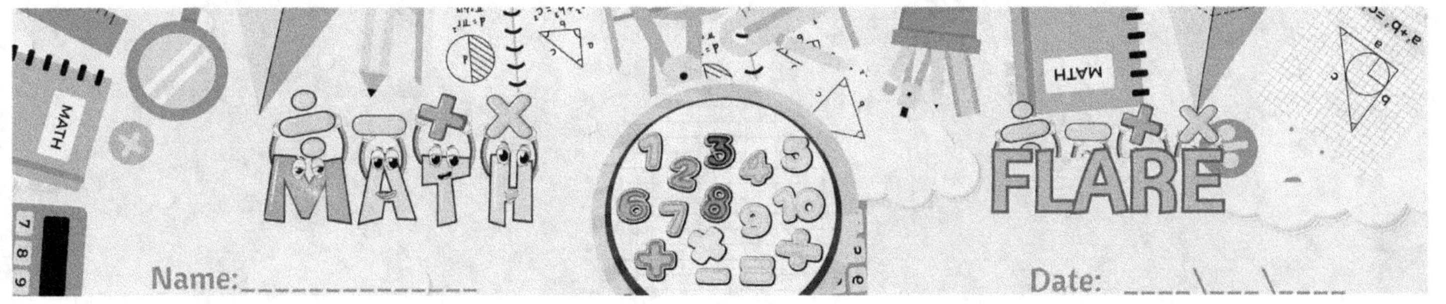

281. 586×304	282. 438×314	283. 214×477	284. 660×672
285. 719×381	286. 435×829	287. 908×746	288. 812×108
289. 166×171	290. 971×446	291. 144×575	292. 233×835

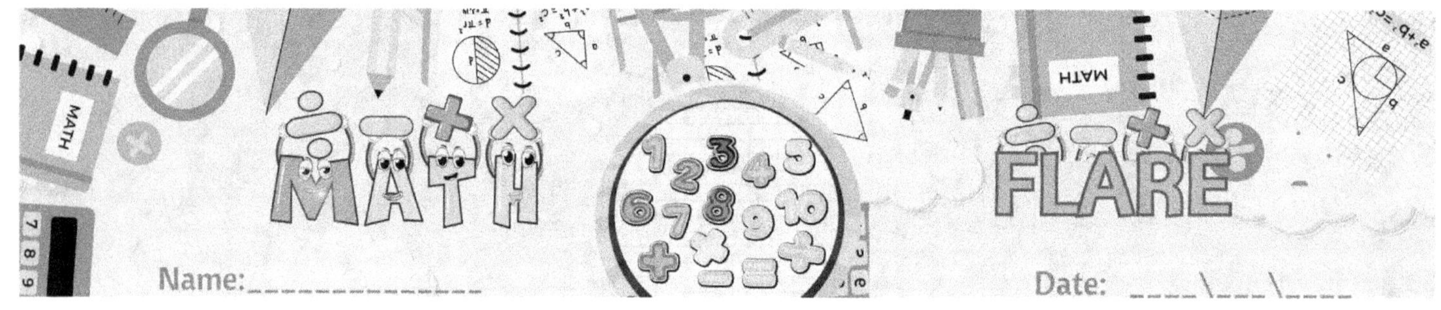

293. 881 × 303	294. 819 × 274	295. 484 × 906	296. 121 × 893
297. 278 × 951	298. 905 × 752	299. 783 × 176	300. 132 × 157
301. 909 × 973	302. 134 × 972	303. 520 × 712	304. 435 × 678

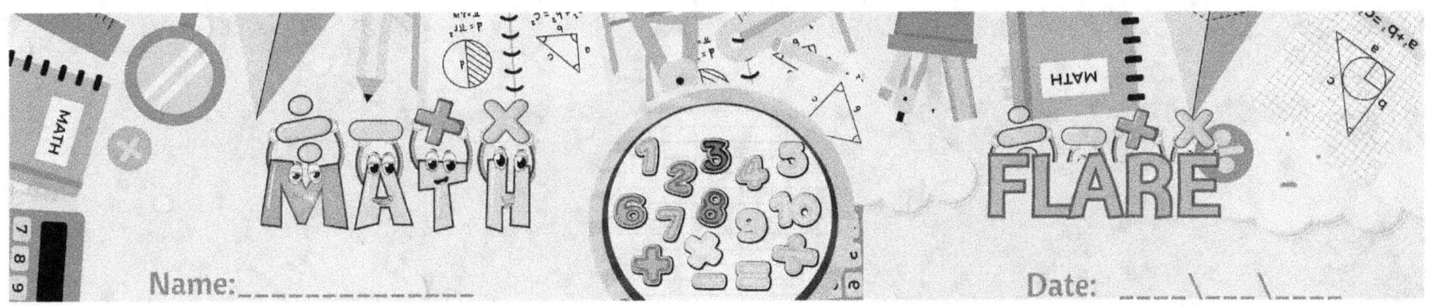

Basic Division

Find the quotient.

305.

$4\overline{)28}$

306.

$3\overline{)12}$

307.

$7\overline{)14}$

308.

$4\overline{)4}$

309.

$2\overline{)12}$

310.

$4\overline{)36}$

311.

$7\overline{)35}$

312.

$3\overline{)24}$

313.

$4\overline{)20}$

314.

$7\overline{)70}$

315.

$8\overline{)16}$

316.

$3\overline{)30}$

317.

$1\overline{)9}$

318.

$5\overline{)10}$

319.

$5\overline{)15}$

320.

$4\overline{)12}$

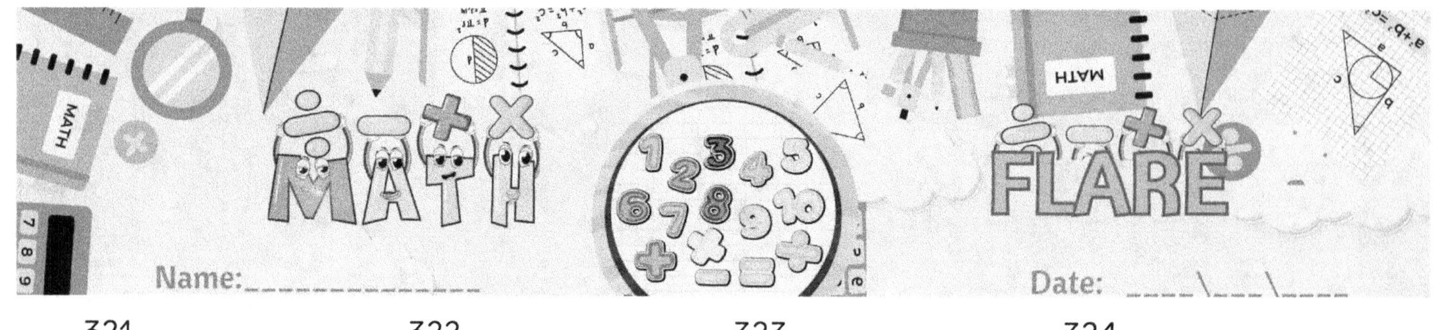

321.

$9\overline{)18}$

322.

$9\overline{)72}$

323.

$7\overline{)56}$

324.

$3\overline{)3}$

325.

$6\overline{)54}$

326.

$7\overline{)21}$

327.

$5\overline{)25}$

328.

$8\overline{)24}$

329.

$2\overline{)10}$

330.

$8\overline{)32}$

331.

$7\overline{)28}$

332.

$3\overline{)9}$

333.

$1\overline{)5}$

334.

$6\overline{)30}$

335.

$4\overline{)24}$

336.

$5\overline{)5}$

337.

$3\overline{)27}$

338.

$5\overline{)20}$

339.

$4\overline{)32}$

340.

$10\overline{)60}$

341. $2\overline{)20}$	342. $9\overline{)36}$	343. $2\overline{)4}$	344. $7\overline{)42}$
345. $9\overline{)45}$	346. $10\overline{)40}$	347. $10\overline{)30}$	348. $5\overline{)40}$
349. $2\overline{)14}$	350. $2\overline{)2}$	351. $3\overline{)21}$	352. $2\overline{)18}$
353. $3\overline{)6}$	354. $6\overline{)42}$	355. $1\overline{)8}$	356. $8\overline{)40}$
357. $2\overline{)8}$	358. $7\overline{)49}$	359. $7\overline{)63}$	360. $2\overline{)16}$

361. $4\overline{)8}$	362. $9\overline{)81}$	363. $6\overline{)60}$	364. $4\overline{)16}$
365. $9\overline{)63}$	366. $4\overline{)40}$	367. $6\overline{)18}$	368. $1\overline{)1}$
369. $6\overline{)48}$	370. $3\overline{)18}$	371. $6\overline{)6}$	372. $9\overline{)27}$
373. $10\overline{)100}$	374. $3\overline{)15}$	375. $9\overline{)54}$	376. $2\overline{)6}$
377. $5\overline{)50}$	378. $8\overline{)8}$	379. $8\overline{)72}$	380. $6\overline{)36}$

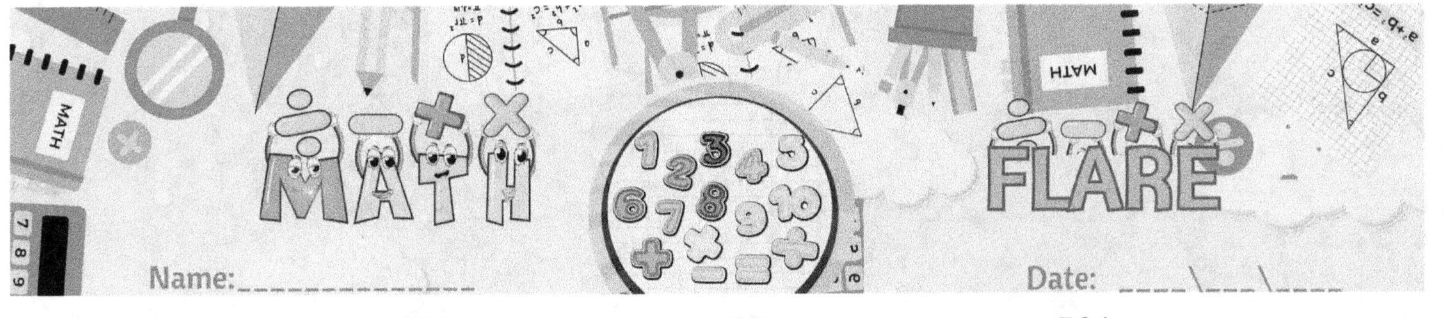

381.	382.	383.	384.
5)30	10)50	10)80	8)80

385.	386.	387.	388.
1)7	1)2	8)48	5)35

389.	390.	391.	392.
7)7	9)9	8)56	1)10

393.	394.	395.	396.
6)12	6)24	10)90	9)90

397.	398.	399.	400.
10)20	8)64	10)10	1)3

Long Division

Find the quotient.

401.

$$8 \overline{)672}$$

402.

$$9 \overline{)315}$$

403.

$$2 \overline{)150}$$

404.

$$7 \overline{)462}$$

405.

$$5 \overline{)455}$$

406.

$$7 \overline{)77}$$

407.

$$7 \overline{)140}$$

408.

$$7 \overline{)378}$$

409.

$$6 \overline{)456}$$

410.

$$12 \overline{)96}$$

411.

$$8 \overline{)72}$$

412.

$$5 \overline{)255}$$

413.

$$3 \overline{)54}$$

414.

$$11 \overline{)847}$$

415.

$$6 \overline{)360}$$

416.

$$8 \overline{)776}$$

417.

$$2 \overline{)178}$$

418.

$$6 \overline{)72}$$

419.

$$4 \overline{)308}$$

420.

$$8 \overline{)560}$$

421.

$$10 \overline{)860}$$

422.

$$8 \overline{)624}$$

423.

$$7 \overline{)525}$$

424.

$$4 \overline{)148}$$

425.

$$7 \overline{)28}$$

426.

$$9 \overline{)324}$$

427.

$$8 \overline{)760}$$

428.

$$8 \overline{)464}$$

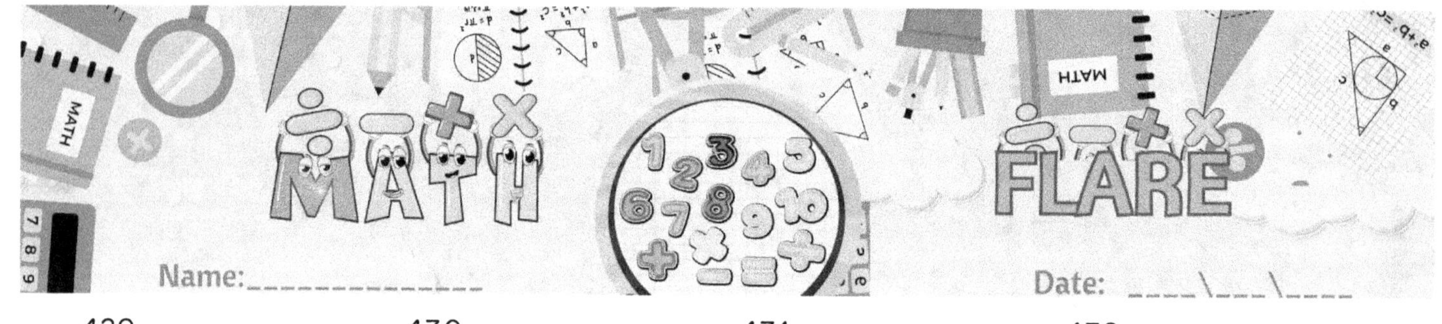

429. $7 \overline{)154}$	430. $3 \overline{)261}$	431. $10 \overline{)800}$	432. $4 \overline{)324}$
433. $4 \overline{)220}$	434. $1 \overline{)63}$	435. $9 \overline{)405}$	436. $4 \overline{)292}$
437. $3 \overline{)90}$	438. $4 \overline{)300}$	439. $6 \overline{)330}$	440. $11 \overline{)473}$
441. $11 \overline{)638}$	442. $3 \overline{)117}$	443. $11 \overline{)341}$	444. $5 \overline{)75}$

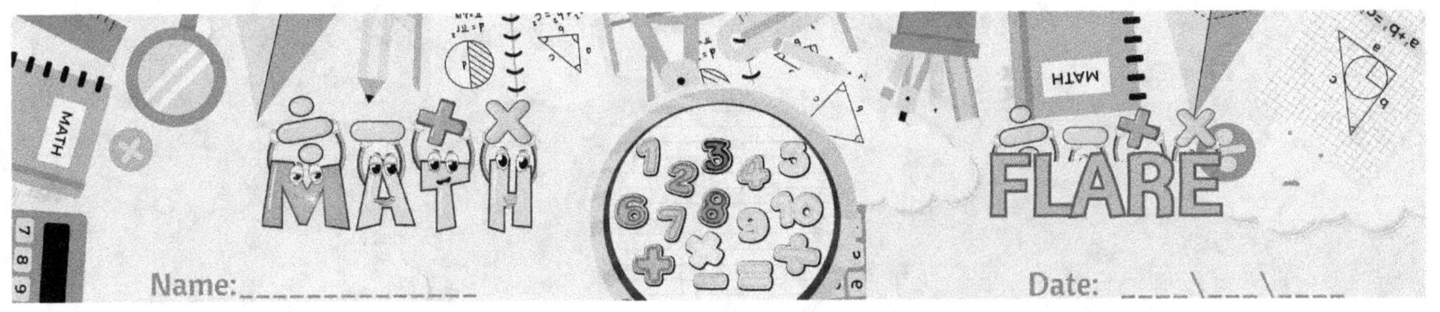

445.

$$4 \overline{)348}$$

446.

$$7 \overline{)49}$$

447.

$$8 \overline{)592}$$

448.

$$11 \overline{)55}$$

449.

$$8 \overline{)648}$$

450.

$$9 \overline{)549}$$

451.

$$8 \overline{)112}$$

452.

$$9 \overline{)900}$$

453.

$$3 \overline{)105}$$

454.

$$9 \overline{)765}$$

455.

$$2 \overline{)196}$$

456.

$$4 \overline{)304}$$

457.

$$11 \overline{)253}$$

458.

$$8 \overline{)688}$$

459.

$$11 \overline{)1,056}$$

460.

$$3 \overline{)258}$$

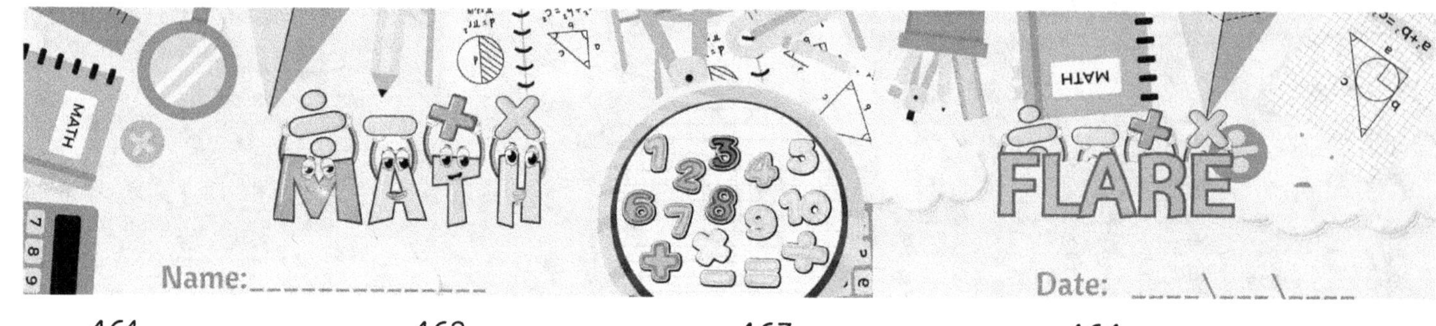

461.

$$5\overline{)440}$$

462.

$$10\overline{)200}$$

463.

$$2\overline{)82}$$

464.

$$5\overline{)100}$$

465.

$$2\overline{)132}$$

466.

$$1\overline{)91}$$

467.

$$8\overline{)272}$$

468.

$$12\overline{)84}$$

469.

$$8\overline{)704}$$

470.

$$2\overline{)198}$$

471.

$$6\overline{)276}$$

472.

$$9\overline{)558}$$

473.

$$10\overline{)840}$$

474.

$$10\overline{)680}$$

475.

$$11\overline{)627}$$

476.

$$10\overline{)900}$$

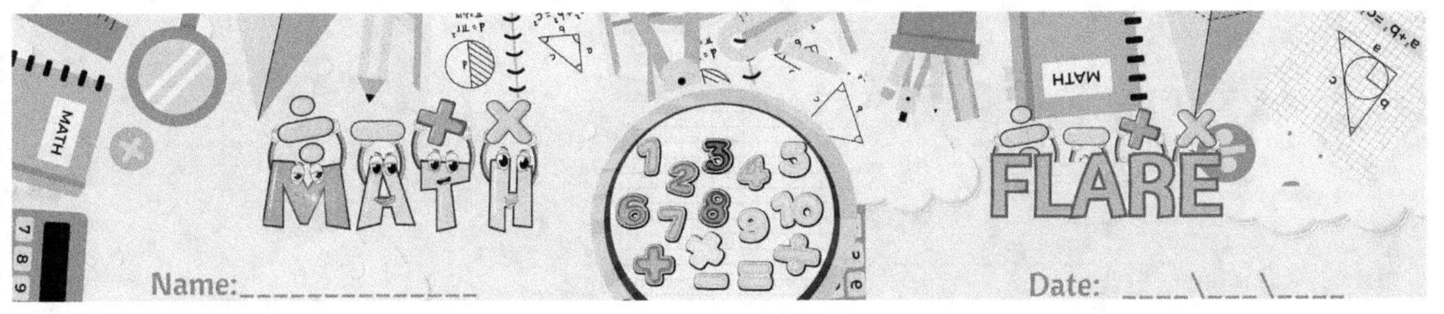

477.

$4\overline{)232}$

478.

$11\overline{)891}$

479.

$11\overline{)583}$

480.

$11\overline{)407}$

481.

$2\overline{)122}$

482.

$4\overline{)28}$

483.

$6\overline{)528}$

484.

$2\overline{)50}$

485.

$6\overline{)180}$

486.

$8\overline{)576}$

487.

$9\overline{)342}$

488.

$10\overline{)470}$

489.

$2\overline{)156}$

490.

$1\overline{)22}$

491.

$10\overline{)40}$

492.

$1\overline{)28}$

493.	494.	495.	496.
$9\overline{)288}$	$8\overline{)344}$	$9\overline{)189}$	$6\overline{)540}$

497.	498.	499.	500.
$7\overline{)574}$	$9\overline{)540}$	$6\overline{)246}$	$8\overline{)24}$

501.	502.	503.	504.
$3\overline{)174}$	$3\overline{)72}$	$8\overline{)392}$	$4\overline{)128}$

505.	506.	507.	508.
$7\overline{)42}$	$9\overline{)198}$	$2\overline{)120}$	$3\overline{)156}$

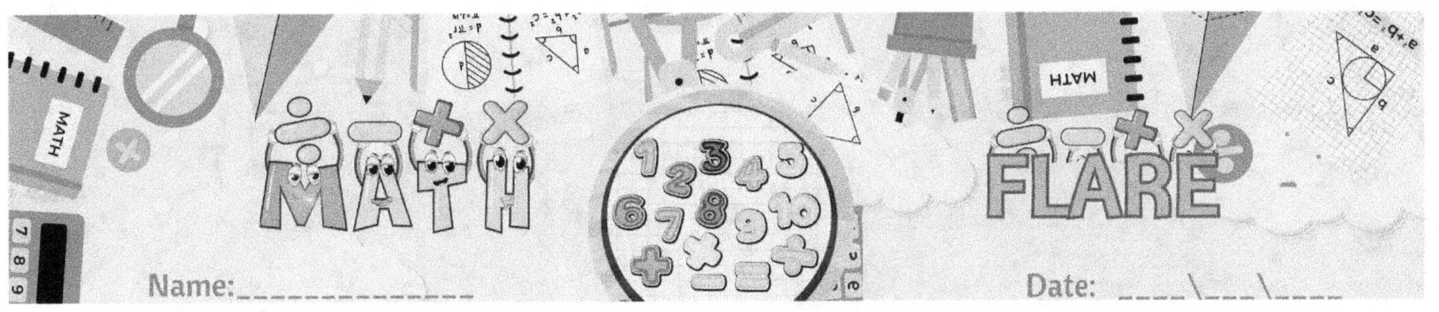

509.

$$3\overline{)240}$$

510.

$$7\overline{)693}$$

511.

$$7\overline{)273}$$

512.

$$4\overline{)344}$$

513.

$$10\overline{)970}$$

514.

$$9\overline{)450}$$

515.

$$4\overline{)256}$$

516.

$$7\overline{)539}$$

517.

$$11\overline{)484}$$

518.

$$2\overline{)160}$$

519.

$$8\overline{)144}$$

520.

$$3\overline{)135}$$

521.

$$8\overline{)296}$$

522.

$$3\overline{)93}$$

523.

$$9\overline{)99}$$

524.

$$6\overline{)570}$$

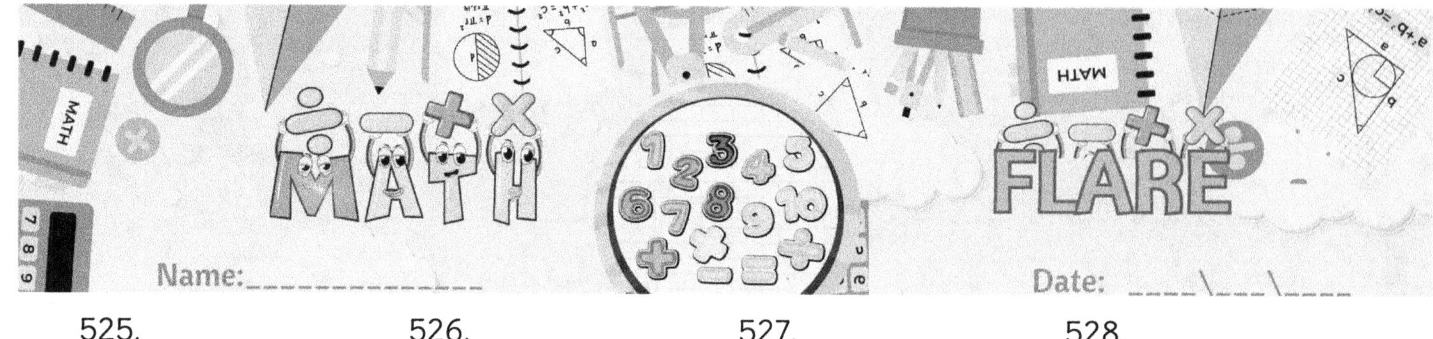

525. $4\overline{)332}$

526. $6\overline{)114}$

527. $2\overline{)166}$

528. $11\overline{)990}$

529. $6\overline{)414}$

530. $9\overline{)711}$

531. $1\overline{)92}$

532. $6\overline{)588}$

533. $5\overline{)310}$

534. $5\overline{)380}$

535. $3\overline{)126}$

536. $10\overline{)90}$

537. $9\overline{)855}$

538. $9\overline{)504}$

539. $3\overline{)201}$

540. $2\overline{)72}$

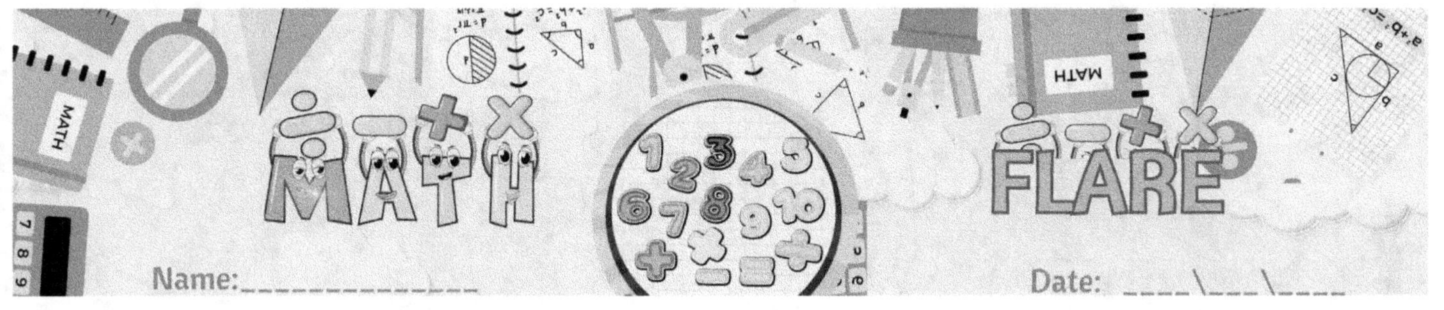

541.

$5\overline{)350}$

542.

$5\overline{)115}$

543.

$11\overline{)275}$

544.

$11\overline{)1,067}$

545.

$6\overline{)222}$

546.

$6\overline{)438}$

547.

$11\overline{)198}$

548.

$12\overline{)192}$

549.

$7\overline{)357}$

550.

$9\overline{)27}$

551.

$5\overline{)485}$

552.

$3\overline{)282}$

553.

$6\overline{)36}$

554.

$9\overline{)594}$

555.

$7\overline{)504}$

556.

$8\overline{)520}$

557.

$$7\overline{)98}$$

558.

$$10\overline{)180}$$

559.

$$12\overline{)588}$$

560.

$$8\overline{)16}$$

561.

$$2\overline{)110}$$

562.

$$8\overline{)56}$$

563.

$$2\overline{)12}$$

564.

$$9\overline{)783}$$

565.

$$2\overline{)64}$$

566.

$$5\overline{)210}$$

567.

$$2\overline{)180}$$

568.

$$2\overline{)192}$$

569.

$$8\overline{)632}$$

570.

$$7\overline{)224}$$

571.

$$11\overline{)286}$$

572.

$$7\overline{)322}$$

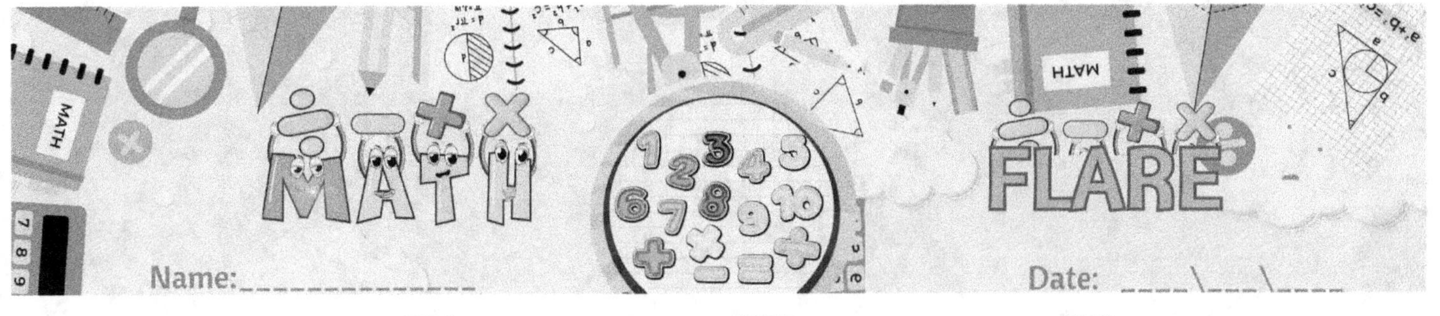

573.

8) 424

574.

2) 170

575.

5) 45

576.

11) 715

577.

5) 215

578.

11) 726

579.

11) 748

580.

3) 183

581.

10) 880

582.

1) 29

583.

3) 255

584.

3) 162

585.

4) 204

586.

2) 14

587.

12) 492

588.

6) 600

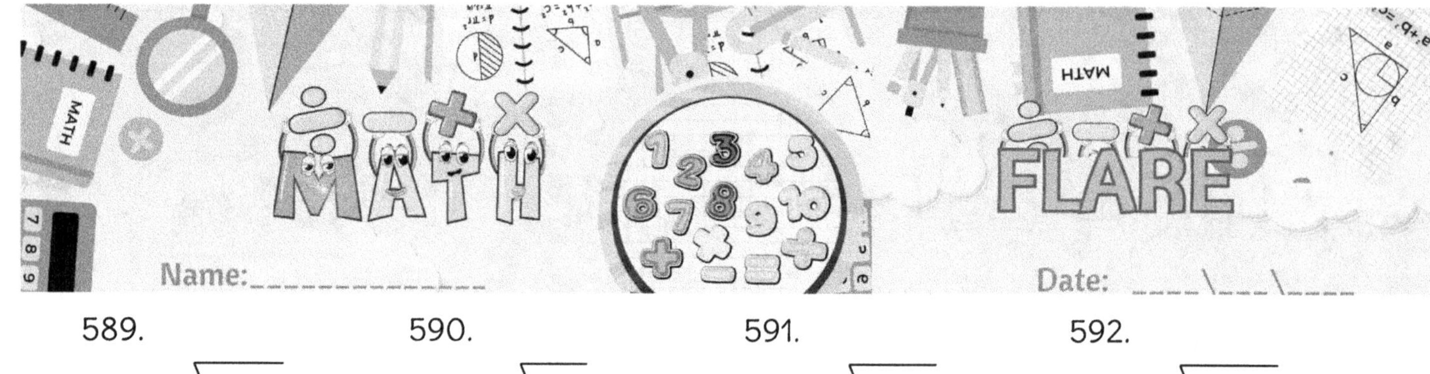

589. 11)‾561‾

590. 1)‾10‾

591. 2)‾182‾

592. 10)‾520‾

593. 1)‾48‾

594. 4)‾20‾

595. 4)‾44‾

596. 2)‾114‾

597. 9)‾117‾

598. 8)‾536‾

599. 4)‾252‾

600. 12)‾408‾

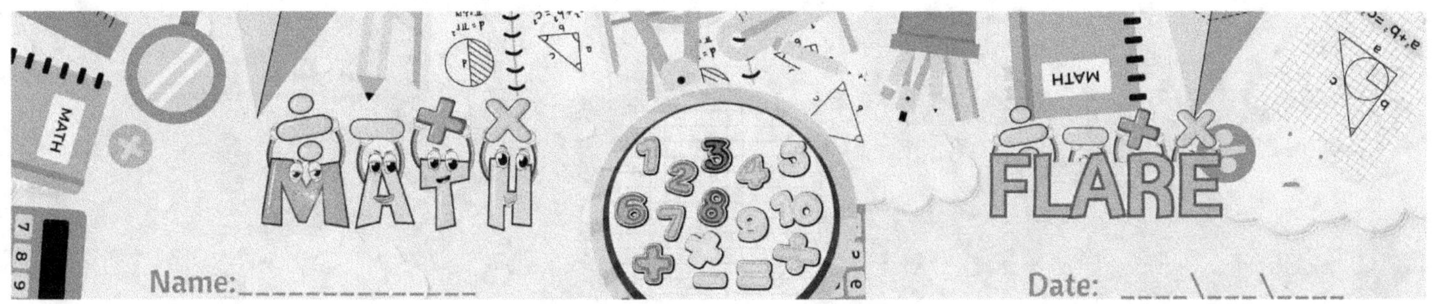

Multiplication Word Problems

601. There are 11 cars in a parking lot. If each car needs two liters of gasoline, how many liters of gasoline are needed for all the cars?

602. Kennedy baked 12 batches of cakes. Each batch had eight cakes. How many cakes did Kennedy bake in all?

603. There are three seats on a bus. If two buses are needed to transport a group of people, how many people can the group consist of at most?

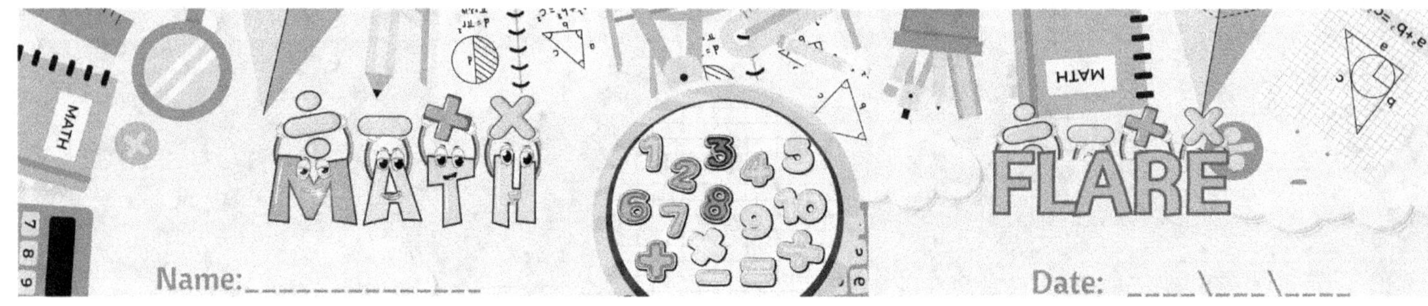

604. There are 15 students in a class. If each student needs 20 pencils, how many pencils are needed for the class in total?

605. There are two bananas in each bunch. If Aurora buys seven bunches, how many bananas will Aurora have?

606. Zachary can solve 15 math problems in one hour. How many math problems can Zachary solve in 17 hours?

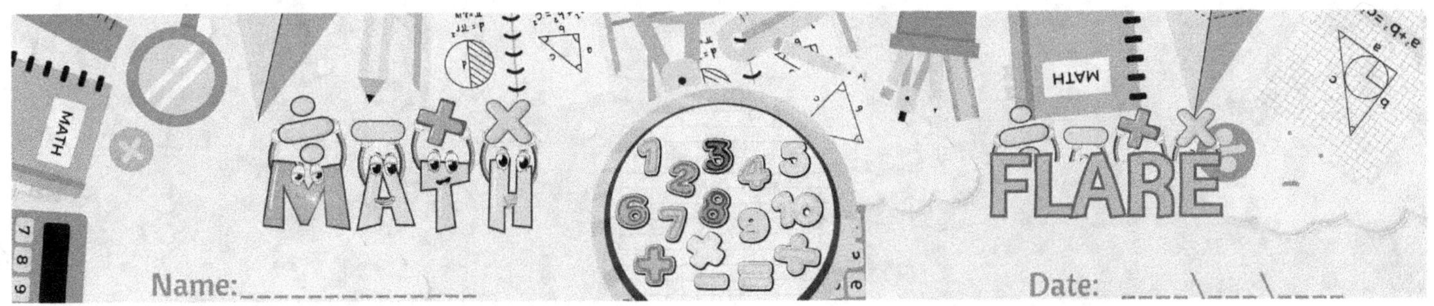

607. Daniel can do 19 pushups in one minute. How many pushups can Daniel do in 11 minutes?

608. Kai sells 12 cakes each day at his bakery. If he works 17 days, how many cakes does he sell?

609. If Ryder can paint 19 square feet of wall in one hour, how many square feet of wall can he paint in two hours?

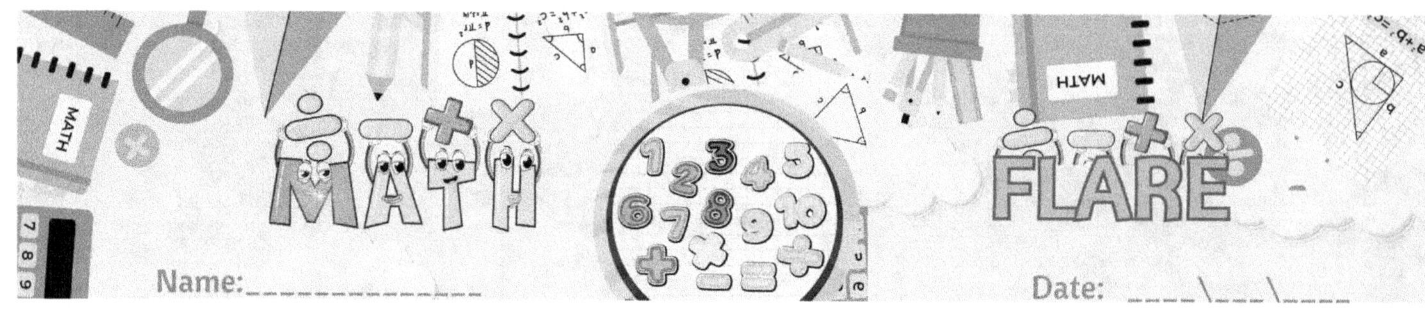

610. Liam can lift eight pounds of weight. How many pounds of weight can Liam lift in total if he lifts for 19 sets?

611. If there are 15 students in each classroom and there are nine classrooms, how many students are there in total?

612. There are 14 slices of pizza in each box. If Ava orders 17 boxes, how many slices of pizza will Ava have?

613. Vincent can catch 16 fish per hour. How many fish can Vincent catch in 11 hours?

614. A movie theater can seat two people. How many people can it seat in seven showings?

615. Madeline has 10 containers of paint. Each container holds 16 liters of paint. How many liters of paint does Madeline have in total?

616. If a boat travels at six miles per hour for seven hours, how far will it go?

617. A box contains 11 bottles of juice, and each bottle contains 10 ounces of juice. How many ounces of juice are there in total?

618. Avery has 15 vases of flowers. Each vase has 17 flowers. How many flowers does Avery have in all?

619. Grace has 19 boxes of cotton swabs. Each box has two cotton swabs. How many cotton swabs does Grace have in all?

620. Arianna baked 16 batches of cookies. Each batch had 18 cookies. How many cookies did Arianna bake in all?

621. Dylan runs six miles per week. How many miles will Dylan run in 15 weeks?

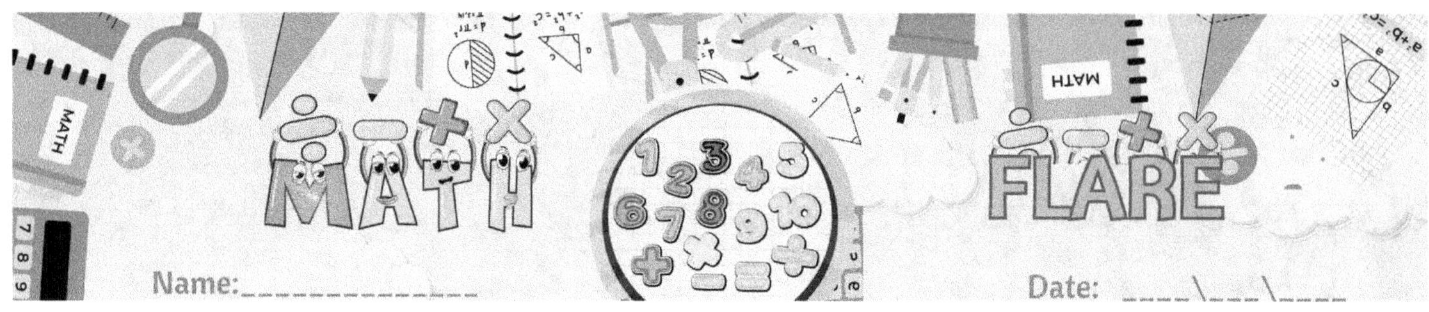

622. Easton runs 11 miles every day. How many miles will Easton run in 13 days?

623. There are nine shelves in Miles's bookcase. 11 books can fit on each shelf. How many books can the bookcase hold in total?

624. David can solve six math problems in one hour. How many problems can David solve in 12 hours?

625. If a car travels at 11 miles per hour for 17 hours, how far will it go?

626. Adalyn has three books. Each book has 12 pages. How many pages does Adalyn have in all?

627. A recipe for a cake calls for three cups of flour. How many cups of flour are needed to make four cakes?

628. A bookshelf can hold 19 books. If there are three bookshelves in a room, how many books can the room hold in total?

629. Serenity wants to make eight flower arrangements, and each arrangement requires 16 flowers. How many flowers does Serenity need in total?

630. Adrian can run 12 laps in 1 hour. How many laps can Adrian run in 12 hour?

Division Word Problems

631. A box of gloves weighs 84 pounds. If one glove weighs two pounds, how many gloves are there in the box?

632. A box contains 372 candy bars. If each candy bar has 12 calories, how many calories are there in the box?

633. If Madeline has 138 bats and wants to distribute them equally to three students, how many bats will each student get?

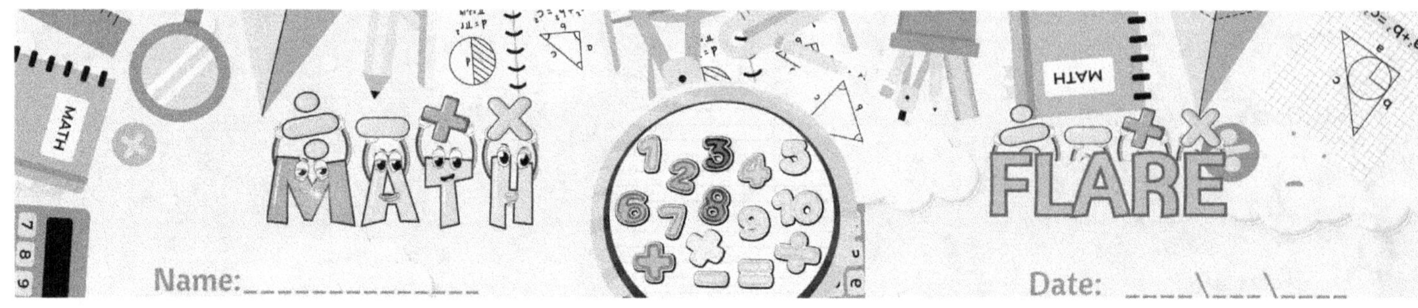

634. Isaac has 357 dollars and wants to buy seven cookies. How much can he spend on each cookies?

635. If the pizzas have 1,241 slices and is divided equally among 17 people, how many slices will each person get?

636. Scarlett has 1,691 cookies and wants to divide them equally into 19 bags. How many cookies will be in each bag?

637. Levi scored 264 points in six games. What is his average score per game?

638. Kinsley has 45 rulers. If Kinsley divides them evenly among 15 children, how many rulers will each child get?

639. Audrey made 95 cookies for a bake sale. She put the cookies in bags, with 19 cookies in each bag. How many bags did she have for the bake sale?

640. You have 234 cups and want to share them equally with nine people. How many cups would each person get?

641. If Mila has 282 lotions and wants to divide them equally among six friends, how many lotions will each friend get?

642. Evelyn is filling up water bottles. Each bottle holds 16 ounces of water. If Evelyn has 1,024 ounces of water, how many water bottles can she fill up?

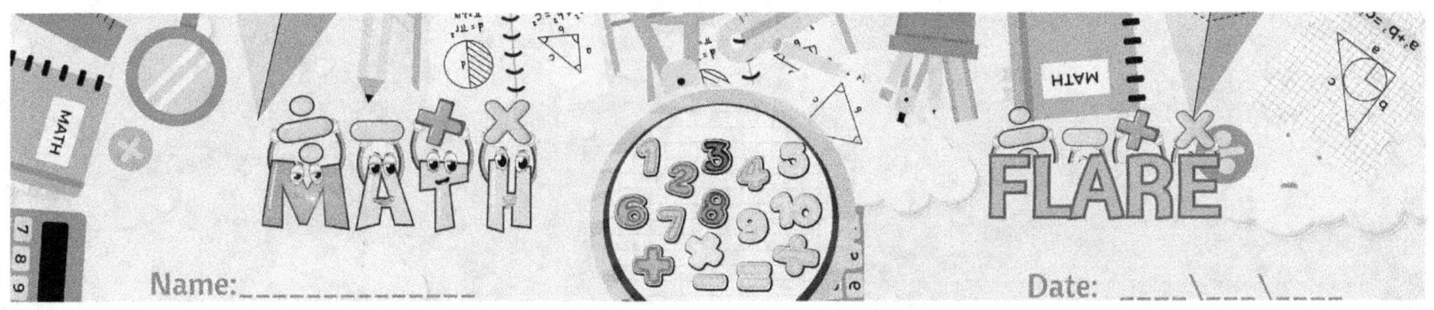

643. If a rope is 952 meters long and you want to cut it into 14 equal pieces, how long will each piece be?

644. If a box contains 215 erasers and each person can have five erasers, how many people can be served from that box?

645. Adam read a book that had 671 pages in 11 days. If he read the same number of pages each day, how many pages did he read per day?

646. Emilia has 150 soaps and wants to divide them equally among 10 children. How many soaps will each child get?

647. Jayden drove 210 miles in 10 hours. What was Jayden's average speed in miles per hour?

648. Skylar has 1,476 radios and wants to divide them equally among 18 people. How many radios will each person get?

649. Victoria is packing 80 cupcakes into boxes. Each box can hold four cupcakes. How many boxes will Victoria need?

650. How many 12 cm pieces of pipe can you cut from a pipe that is 1,164 cm long?

651. Luna has $450 and she wants to buy six thermometers that cost the same amount. How much does each thermometers cost?

652. At a restaurant, 15 friends decided to divide the bill equally. If each person paid $81, then what was the total bill?

653. If a field is 378 acres and it is divided into 18 equal parts, how many acres is each part?

654. If a garden is 462 feet long and it is divided into seven equal parts, how long is each part?

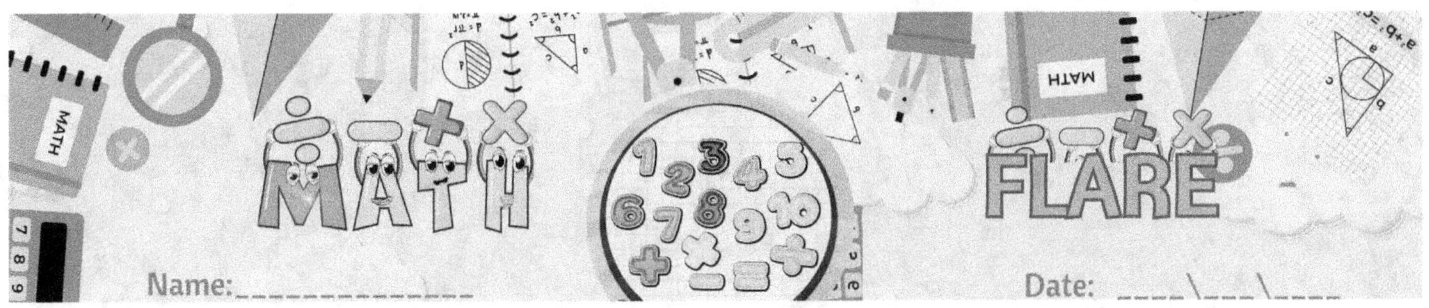

655. It takes Sofia 91 minutes to write 1 page. How many pages can Sofia write in 819 minutes?

656. A book has 160 chapters. If you want to read the book in five days, how many chapters do you need to read per day?

657. A pool is 306 meters long. If it is divided into nine equal parts, how long is each part?

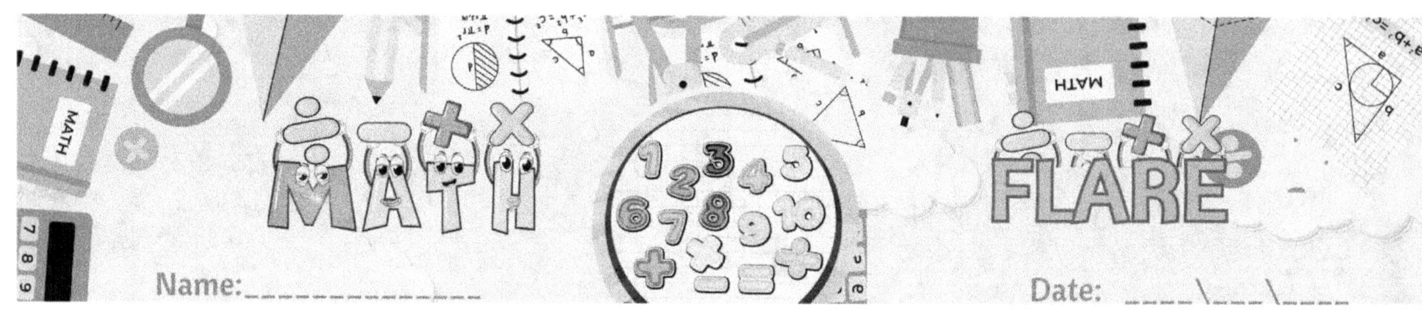

658. A car can travel 448 miles on eight gallons of gas. How many miles can it travel on 1 gallon of gas?

659. A recipe calls for 1,209 cups of sugar to make 13 cookies. How much sugar is needed to make 1 cookie?

660. A box of gloves has 520 gloves. If 13 children each get an equal number of gloves, how many gloves will each child get?

ANSWERS

Page 1: Multiplication: 2 x 1

1. 32	2. 96	3. 22	4. 35	5. 88	6. 44	7. 82	8. 84
9. 40	10. 46	11. 86	12. 48	13. 50	14. 38	15. 63	16. 20
17. 88	18. 55	19. 39	20. 40	21. 62	22. 30	23. 68	24. 90
25. 69	26. 80	27. 42	28. 36	29. 44	30. 89	31. 22	32. 44
33. 66	34. 24	35. 64	36. 26	37. 60	38. 48	39. 46	40. 13

Page 3: Multiplication: 3 x 1

41. 806	42. 206	43. 624	44. 246	45. 104	46. 393	47. 880
48. 484	49. 555	50. 639	51. 132	52. 146	53. 969	54. 609
55. 670	56. 237	57. 448	58. 390	59. 484	60. 844	61. 500
62. 888	63. 888	64. 963	65. 404	66. 440	67. 635	68. 464
69. 648	70. 800	71. 369	72. 282	73. 884	74. 966	75. 630
76. 424	77. 303	78. 360	79. 404	80. 396		

Page 5: Multiplication: 4 x 1

81. 8,404	82. 4,628	83. 3,000	84. 4,842	85. 4,808
86. 7,332	87. 4,880	88. 8,262	89. 4,172	90. 4,888
91. 8,248	92. 4,080	93. 5,984	94. 9,870	95. 4,404
96. 3,006	97. 8,488	98. 8,020	99. 4,840	100. 8,840
101. 8,084	102. 8,844	103. 6,069	104. 5,055	105. 3,033
106. 4,246	107. 5,500	108. 3,339	109. 2,460	110. 3,930

| 111. 3,993 | 112. 6,802 | 113. 5,000 | 114. 4,480 | 115. 6,066 |
| 116. 4,686 | 117. 8,408 | 118. 8,084 | 119. 4,428 | 120. 8,688 |

Page 7: Multiplication (double Digit)

121. 816	122. 1,066	123. 276	124. 1,036	125. 625
126. 3,430	127. 7,426	128. 3,479	129. 4,312	130. 2,805
131. 1,458	132. 3,256	133. 4,030	134. 1,020	135. 4,186
136. 693	137. 1,927	138. 6,630	139. 676	140. 5,698
141. 2,583	142. 1,088	143. 3,306	144. 546	145. 2,832
146. 3,216	147. 1,485	148. 1,196	149. 2,736	150. 1,323
151. 1,496	152. 2,808	153. 364	154. 2,079	155. 6,510
156. 938	157. 247	158. 5,865	159. 627	160. 468
161. 918	162. 3,402	163. 5,616	164. 1,456	165. 3,496
166. 1,184	167. 1,225	168. 4,928	169. 795	170. 1,260
171. 1,938	172. 2,464	173. 5,733	174. 810	175. 2,268
176. 4,410	177. 418	178. 7,840	179. 3,255	180. 410
181. 800	182. 420	183. 5,888	184. 6,006	185. 690
186. 6,320	187. 7,304	188. 7,719	189. 1,190	190. 1,250
191. 3,589	192. 357	193. 1,664	194. 1,638	195. 648
196. 651				

Page 12: Multiplication (3 Digit)

| 197. 468,503 | 198. 301,359 | 199. 95,748 | 200. 221,662 |

201. 578,158   202. 631,840   203. 413,574   204. 281,610

205. 51,040   206. 286,700   207. 454,860   208. 31,746

209. 80,640   210. 182,850   211. 244,053   212. 112,488

213. 637,755   214. 37,944   215. 557,480   216. 477,116

217. 467,360   218. 271,656   219. 89,892   220. 315,252

221. 273,996   222. 288,470   223. 27,104   224. 455,600

225. 170,046   226. 122,672   227. 502,944   228. 233,800

229. 199,143   230. 607,959   231. 468,833   232. 339,852

233. 159,639   234. 47,616   235. 253,236   236. 110,125

237. 230,868   238. 63,245   239. 212,290   240. 881,400

241. 82,017   242. 131,325   243. 199,892   244. 232,677

245. 127,506   246. 230,888   247. 648,396   248. 102,835

249. 333,324   250. 771,420   251. 476,256   252. 102,879

253. 144,255   254. 89,830   255. 421,057   256. 598,703

257. 705,939   258. 689,318   259. 204,036   260. 183,260

261. 104,880   262. 159,896   263. 632,040   264. 160,710

265. 292,984   266. 134,562   267. 86,215   268. 127,697

269. 450,252   270. 215,058   271. 212,454   272. 95,940

273. 304,380   274. 486,438   275. 302,670   276. 186,448

277. 96,702   278. 270,100   279. 307,300   280. 281,394

281. 178,144   282. 137,532   283. 102,078   284. 443,520

285. 273,939   286. 360,615   287. 677,368   288. 87,696

289. 28,386   290. 433,066   291. 82,800   292. 194,555

293. 266,943   294. 224,406   295. 438,504   296. 108,053

297. 264,378   298. 680,560   299. 137,808   300. 20,724

301. 884,457   302. 130,248   303. 370,240   304. 294,930

Page 21:   Basic Division

305. 7   306. 4   307. 2   308. 1   309. 6   310. 9   311. 5   312. 8

313. 5   314. 10   315. 2   316. 10   317. 9   318. 2   319. 3   320. 3

321. 2   322. 8   323. 8   324. 1   325. 9   326. 3   327. 5   328. 3

329. 5   330. 4   331. 4   332. 3   333. 5   334. 5   335. 6   336. 1

337. 9   338. 4   339. 8   340. 6   341. 10   342. 4   343. 2   344. 6

345. 5   346. 4   347. 3   348. 8   349. 7   350. 1   351. 7   352. 9

353. 2   354. 7   355. 8   356. 5   357. 4   358. 7   359. 9   360. 8

361. 2   362. 9   363. 10   364. 4   365. 7   366. 10   367. 3   368. 1

369. 8   370. 6   371. 1   372. 3   373. 10   374. 5   375. 6   376. 3

377. 10   378. 1   379. 9   380. 6   381. 6   382. 5   383. 8   384. 10

385. 7   386. 2   387. 6   388. 7   389. 1   390. 1   391. 7   392. 10

393. 2   394. 4   395. 9   396. 10   397. 2   398. 8   399. 1   400. 3

Page 26:   Long Division

401. 84   402. 35   403. 75   404. 66   405. 91   406. 11

407. 20   408. 54   409. 76   410. 8   411. 9   412. 51

413. 18	414. 77	415. 60	416. 97	417. 89	418. 12
419. 77	420. 70	421. 86	422. 78	423. 75	424. 37
425. 4	426. 36	427. 95	428. 58	429. 22	430. 87
431. 80	432. 81	433. 55	434. 63	435. 45	436. 73
437. 30	438. 75	439. 55	440. 43	441. 58	442. 39
443. 31	444. 15	445. 87	446. 7	447. 74	448. 5
449. 81	450. 61	451. 14	452. 100	453. 35	454. 85
455. 98	456. 76	457. 23	458. 86	459. 96	460. 86
461. 88	462. 20	463. 41	464. 20	465. 66	466. 91
467. 34	468. 7	469. 88	470. 99	471. 46	472. 62
473. 84	474. 68	475. 57	476. 90	477. 58	478. 81
479. 53	480. 37	481. 61	482. 7	483. 88	484. 25
485. 30	486. 72	487. 38	488. 47	489. 78	490. 22
491. 4	492. 28	493. 32	494. 43	495. 21	496. 90
497. 82	498. 60	499. 41	500. 3	501. 58	502. 24
503. 49	504. 32	505. 6	506. 22	507. 60	508. 52
509. 80	510. 99	511. 39	512. 86	513. 97	514. 50
515. 64	516. 77	517. 44	518. 80	519. 18	520. 45
521. 37	522. 31	523. 11	524. 95	525. 83	526. 19
527. 83	528. 90	529. 69	530. 79	531. 92	532. 98
533. 62	534. 76	535. 42	536. 9	537. 95	538. 56

539. 67	540. 36	541. 70	542. 23	543. 25	544. 97
545. 37	546. 73	547. 18	548. 16	549. 51	550. 3
551. 97	552. 94	553. 6	554. 66	555. 72	556. 65
557. 14	558. 18	559. 49	560. 2	561. 55	562. 7
563. 6	564. 87	565. 32	566. 42	567. 90	568. 96
569. 79	570. 32	571. 26	572. 46	573. 53	574. 85
575. 9	576. 65	577. 43	578. 66	579. 68	580. 61
581. 88	582. 29	583. 85	584. 54	585. 51	586. 7
587. 41	588. 100	589. 51	590. 10	591. 91	592. 52
593. 48	594. 5	595. 11	596. 57	597. 13	598. 67
599. 63	600. 34				

Page 39: Multiplication Word Problems

601. 22	602. 96	603. 6	604. 300	605. 14	606. 255
607. 209	608. 204	609. 38	610. 152	611. 135	612. 238
613. 176	614. 14	615. 160	616. 42	617. 110	618. 255
619. 38	620. 288	621. 90	622. 143	623. 99	624. 72
625. 187	626. 36	627. 12	628. 57	629. 128	630. 144

Page 49: Division Word Problems

631. 42	632. 31	633. 46	634. 51	635. 73	636. 89
637. 44	638. 3	639. 5	640. 26	641. 47	642. 64
643. 68	644. 43	645. 61	646. 15	647. 21	648. 82

649. 20   650. 97   651. 75   652. 1,215   653. 21   654. 66

655. 9   656. 32   657. 34   658. 56   659. 93   660. 40